let's travel in
MEXICO

Edited by Darlene Geis

A TRAVEL PRESS BOOK

PICTURE ACKNOWLEDGMENTS
The full-color illustrations in this book are the work of the following photographers and artists whose collaboration is gratefully acknowledged. Photographed in Mexico by Orville Goldner (4, 6, 15, 18, 19, 25, 30, 31); Marvin Becker (5, 9, 10, 14, 20, 21, 23, 24, 28); Ursula Toomey (2, 3, 11, 16, 26); Herbert Lanks (12, 27); P.I.P. (7, 8, 13, 17, 22, 29); Freelance Photographers Guild (1, 32). For the black-and-white photographs we wish to thank Orville Goldner; Hamilton Wright; Patrice Hartley and Bernard Silberstein from Rapho-Guillumette; Three Lions; Photo Researchers. The map was made by Enrico Arno.

CONTENTS

UNITED STATES

LOWER CALIFORNIA

Gulf of California

Nogales

Ciudad Juárez

Nuevo Laredo

SIERRA MADRE OCCIDENTAL

SIERRA MADRE ORIENTAL

PACIFIC

28

27

32

Tula 1

23-26

Pátzcuaro

Mexico City

6-13

Teotihuacán 4

29 Tlaxcala

5

IZTACCIHUATL

19

Xochimilco

Cuernavaca

POPOCATEPETL

20
21

Puebla

14-18

Taxco

22 Acapulco

30

Oaxaca

31

Tlacolula

OCEAN

OF AMERICA

Reforma

8

9

6
7

11

10

Insurgentes

Av. Baja California

Av. Central

Calz. de San Antonio Abad.

Avenida de los

MEXICO CITY

12

13

GULF OF MEXICO

Mérida

2

YUCATAN

Chichén Itzá

3

GUATEMALA

BR. HOND.

HONDURAS

Locales of thirty-two full-page pictures

MEXICO,
COUNTRY OF COLOR
AND CONTRAST

THE sunny land called Mexico is vivid and picturesque. It is a land that is predominately Indian with overtones of colonial Spanish. Its ways are unique and strange. It is this very strangeness of Mexico that makes travel there such an exciting adventure.

Mexico curves like a great horn below the United States. The broad, flaring top of the horn lies along the southern borders of California, Arizona, New Mexico and Texas. About halfway down, the horn narrows and hooks to the east, where it points up into the Gulf of Mexico. That point is the peninsula of Yucatán. Hanging down from the broad top of the horn into the Pacific Ocean is the long peninsula of Lower California. The entire country is less than one-quarter the size of the United States.

Two great coastal ranges, the Sierra Madre (SYEHR-*ah* MAH-*dreh*) Occidental and the Sierra Madre Oriental (or the Mother Range of the West and of the East), embrace the broad high tableland of north central Mexico. It is on this tableland that the greater number of Mexico's 30,000,000 people live, their horizons hemmed by mountains. Just below Mexico City, where the horn begins to narrow, the ranges come together in a disorder of mountains and valleys. The snow-capped cones of the twin volcanoes, Popocatépetl (*poh-poh-kah-*TEH*-pet'l*), or the Mountain That Smokes, and Iztaccihuatl (*ees-tahk-*SEE*-what'l*), or the White Lady, point 17,000 feet into the sky, dominating this mountainous jumble.

The geography of Mexico was best described by her Spanish conqueror Hernán Cortés (*err-*NAHN *kor-*TESS). When the King of Spain asked him what Mexico looked like, Cortés is said to have crushed a piece of paper between his hands. Then he laid the crumpled surface before his king and replied, "Like that, your Majesty." Cortés knew the answer only too well from having marched over much of that difficult land in order to subdue its Indian population.

THE INDIAN HERITAGE

Ancient Indians live again in these proud descendants of a gifted race.

Before the white man came to America it was inhabited by a copper-skinned people who had discovered it about 20,000 years earlier. It is believed that they passed across the Bering Strait from Asia to Alaska and traveled down into the Americas. Some of them had remarkable civilizations. The Mayans (MAH-*yans*), whose pyramids and temples we will see in Yucatán, knew astronomy, engineering and mathematics, and had an unchanging 365-day calendar even more accurate than those of the Greeks and Romans. The Mayans were magnificent artists and craftsmen, and have aptly been called "The Greeks of the New World."

The Toltecs were another group of Indians who lived before history was recorded. They left the ruins of their flourishing culture in Mexico, too. But many of the Mexican Indians fell under the domination of the warlike Aztecs who organized and ruled Mexico for two hundred years, until Cortés and the Spaniards came and conquered them in the sixteenth century.

The Mexican Indians today carry many traces of their Aztec ancestry. The love of flowers and brilliant color, the patterns and designs of their handicrafts, and their wonderful faces with broad cheekbones and deep-set eyes are certainly a heritage from Aztec forebears. Even the name of the country, "Mexico," comes from the name of the Aztec people, the Mexica. And Mexico City, the modern capital, rises from the site of the old Aztec capital, Tenochtitlán (*teh-noch-tee-*TLAHN). An Aztec legend tells how the city was founded. The nomadic Indians were looking for a place to settle, and their war god, Mexitl, told them not to stop until they found the place where they would see an eagle perched on a cactus, eating a snake. That seemed like a fairly impossible combination, but on one of the islands of Lake Texcoco (*tehs-*KOH-*koh*) there were a cactus, an eagle and a snake just as the god had described them. You can see them today on the Mexican flag and on many of the coins of the Republic. The Mexican emblem was taken from this old legend. The Aztecs settled on Lake Texcoco and built a fabulous capital on the islands, connected by causeways to the mainland. When Cortés and the Spaniards first came upon this city after their difficult march across the mountains, they thought it was an enchanted place rising out of the water like a mirage.

Aside from the treasures of gold and silver that the Spaniards took from the Aztecs, there were strange new foods—Indian corn, sweet potatoes, chocolate and peppers that found their way to the Old World as a result of the conquest. We are indebted to the Mexican Indians for two rather questionable habits—smoking and gum-chewing. Tobacco was a crop unknown in Europe, but cultivated in Mexico. And in Yucatán the gummy sap of the sapodilla tree is called chicle, and is the chief ingredient of chewing gum.

Although the Spaniards conquered Mexico, the Indian and his ways have been dominant in the country. Even now, at least fifty per cent of the people in Mexico are purely or partly Indian and still observe many Indian customs.

THE SPANISH INFLUENCE

The stamp of the Spanish conquest is strong upon the land, although it has been imprinted on an Indian civilization. The Spanish missionaries smashed the idols and tore down the temples of pagan belief. But they immediately supplanted them with saints and churches. The new religion was Christianity— and the conversion of the

This patio is cloistered and peaceful—a Spanish oasis in an alien land.

11

Mexican folk dancers stamp out the rhythms of a gay dance borrowed from old Spain.

natives was made easier by building churches on old temple sites, and making images of the saints with Indian features and coloring. The Indians' love of song and dance and festival was encouraged in the numerous *fiestas* that give Mexican worship its distinctiveness.

But the most striking imprint of the Spanish conquest is to be found in the cities and towns of Mexico. Each is a model Spanish town with a central plaza, fountains, towered church and buildings in the Spanish style. And yet these towns are unmistakably Mexican and not Spanish. The mountains, the brilliant flowers, the colorful Indian decorations proclaim that this is Mexico. And if that were not enough, the people in the streets and sauntering around the plaza would tell you so at once. The broad-brimmed Spanish hat has become a Mexican sombrero; the mantilla (*mahn-*TEEL*-yah*) has become a *rebozo* (*reh-*BOH*-so*); the brightly striped serape (*seh-*RAH*-peh*) is distinctly Mexican; and the Indian sandal has evolved into the comfortable *huarache* (*hwah-*RAH*-cheh*).

12

MODERN MEXICO

The Mexican government, too, has had its evolution—usually by revolution. In this country of volcanoes and earthquakes, society's adjustments have frequently taken the form of equally violent eruptions or shake-ups. Mexico's history has been punctuated with bloodshed and revolution. On September 16, 1810, Mexico proclaimed its independence. Yet there have been numerous reforms, revolutions, and two brief monarchies since that date. A new constitution was adopted in 1917, and since then the Mexican government has been more stabile.

Mexico has made tremendous strides in the past forty years. She is a country of vast natural resources—far more than the gold and silver that inflamed the greed of Cortés and his men. There are important oil and mining industries, machinery, textiles, chemicals, plastics and electrical equipment—all playing a part in the industrialization of the country.

When we see Mexico City with its broad avenues humming with traffic and its modern glass skyscrapers, we realize that there is more to this country than the stereotyped picture of the Mexican snoozing under his sombrero in the shadow of a cactus. On the other hand, down these same broad avenues walks an occasional barefoot peasant—only one Mexican in three wears shoes—and we realize that the country still has a way to go.

TRAVEL IN MEXICO

In recent years Americans have been visiting their southern neighbor at the rate of 500,000 a year. For the most part they come by air or by automobile. Air travel makes it possible to get to many heretofore inaccessible towns. The excellent highways—West Coast, Central and Pan American—enable the tourist to travel from town to town and still get the feel of the country in between. For those hardy souls who enjoy mountain driving and hairpin curves, the new highways are a boon.

The climate is remarkable. It has less to do with seasons than with altitude. Near sea level the land is green and lush and can be steamily tropical. Up on the high tableland, Monterrey, for example, is an arid desert country, yet because of its altitude it does not get unbearably hot. There are parts of Mexico where in a few hours' time you can drop from cool pine forests to the tropical profusion of orchids and banana plantations.

The rainy season in Central Mexico lasts from June through September. Then the country is green and brilliant, though the rain regularly holds off until late afternoon. During the winter dry season, the land is

13

brown and the air is mild and clear and sparkling. In other words you can visit Mexico at any time of year and still find the climate and scenery you prefer.

The various sections of Mexico have distinct personalities, too. The little border towns of Tijuana (*tee-*HWAH*-nah*), Nogales (*noh-*GAH*-less*), Juárez (HWAH*-ress*), Nuevo Laredo (NWEH*-voh lah-*REH*-doh*) are for the quick tourist who wants to buy gimcrack souvenirs, gamble and hurry home again. Mexico City is for the cosmopolite. Acapulco (*ah-kah-*POOL*-koh*) is for the resort-lover. Baja (BAH*-hah*), or Lower, California is for the fisherman who likes the rugged life. Yucatán, with its jungles enclosing the Mayan mysteries, is for the adventurous and intellectually curious. There is something for everybody in this country of contrasts. And as the Spanish saying puts it, "Once the dust of Mexico has settled on your heart, you have no rest in any other land."

So let's be up and traveling, and we will see a part of America whose fascinating civilization flourished long before Columbus discovered this continent.

The modern bus terminal in Guadalajara is a symbol of the new era of travel in Mexico.

let's travel in

MEXICO

DANCERS
AT TULA:
WHERE THE OLD
GODS STILL STAND

WE HAVE crossed the border into Mexico and here, as we can see, is a different world. Ancient America stares from the faces of the great stone gods that stood like this beneath the hot Mexican sun a thousand years ago. We are in the town of Tula (TOO-*lah*), about forty-five miles north of Mexico City, where archaeologists have unearthed the remains of an old civilization. The Toltecs (TOHL-*teks*), an Indian people who flourished about the tenth century A.D., built their capital at Tula, and ruins of their pyramids, a ball court and these striking sculptures have recently been found here.

The Toltec pyramids are remarkable not only because they indicate that these early people had an amazing knowledge of structural engineering; they must also have been able to make precise astronomical measurements. For the pyramids were built in such a way that the sun's rays would strike a planned point on certain days of the year. This surpasses European sundials that merely recorded the hours of the day.

By the time the Spaniards came to Mexico under the leadership of Cortés, this highly developed culture had all but vanished, and the military Aztecs dominated the land. In this picture we see an Aztec dance that re-enacts the story of the conquest, performed before statues that were old and forgotten when the conquest took place. Costumed in brilliant feathers, these descendants of Aztec warriors dance as their ancestors used to on religious holidays. But their religion now is Christian rather than pagan, and they have given the tragic story of their overthrow a happy ending. When they do this dance at a saint's day *fiesta,* they celebrate the fact that the heathen Aztecs were brought to salvation by their Christian conquerors. Mexican folk music and art still proclaim the color, beauty and joy of life inherited from the pagan past, and watching these dancers we catch a glimpse of America as it was before the white man came.

MAYAN FAMILY: DESCENDANTS OF AN ANCIENT RACE

IN REMOTE Yucatán we find the Mayas, whose forebears merged with the Toltecs to become the most highly civilized people of the New World. Today the Mayas of all social classes speak their own ancient language and have customs and dress that set them apart from other Mexicans. These small but sturdy people have a calm archaic beauty and their faces are seen again and again in the sculpture on old Mayan ruins.

This Mayan family, sitting for its portrait against a background of lush jungle greenery, is typical. Although there is little water in Yucatán, the people manage to keep themselves scrupulously clean—a characteristic not shared with all other Mexican Indians. The women wear a white, square-necked tunic called a huipil (*we*-PEEL), heavily embroidered in vivid colors. Both men and women have special garments of finer material and more elaborate design for Sundays and feast days.

Dancing on an ancient altar of sacrifice, these Mayan women bring to life the glory of Chichén Itzá.

Love of beauty and pride of origin make native Mexican costumes works of art. The extravagantly adorned and colorful clothes hark back to the times when the Indians ruled the land and dressed in barbaric splendor. Poor as they are now, and meager as their material possessions may be, the people of every village still adorn themselves in clothes whose workmanship bears the stamp of native artistry. It is the heritage, carried over into daily life, of a once proud civilization.

PYRAMID IN YUCATAN: TEMPLE OF SPLENDID SYMMETRY

DEEP in the green jungles of Yucatán stand the ruins of Chichén Itzá (*chee*-CHAIN *it*-SAH), a city that the Mayans and Toltecs had abandoned nearly a hundred years before the Spaniards came. By the time Cortés arrived in Mexico, the jungle had crept over the deserted buildings, hiding them in a green tangle, and the Mayan civilization was but a whisper and a myth to the Spaniards.

Now the jungle has been cleared and the buildings laid bare for us to marvel at. We are looking across a broad terrace to El Castillo (*ehl kahs*-TEEL-*yoh*), The Castle, a pyramid temple built to honor the feathered-serpent god known as Quetzalcoatl (*ket-sahl*-KOH-*t'l*). The remarkable buildings of this ceremonial center were made of stone and stucco, and their noble proportions dwarfed the simple little adobe huts where the ordinary Mayan people lived. How the Mayans were able to do such fine stonework is a puzzle, because they had no metal tools and had to use cutting implements made of sharpened rock.

But the most amazing thing about this temple is its mathematical precision. On all four sides of the pyramid are steep stairways, ninety-one steps high. This adds up to three hundred and sixty-four, and the landing at the top makes the total three hundred and sixty-five, or the number of days in the Mayan year. Obviously their religion was much concerned with the sun, moon and stars and the planetary cycles. For the Mayans were an agricultural people whose religion and calendar evolved from a need to know when to sow and when to reap.

We can imagine this city in the days of its glory, when priests robed in brilliant feather cloaks and hung with jaguar skins led processions up the stairway of the pyramid. Their god was a cruel one demanding human sacrifices, but in spite of all they did to appease him, their crops eventually failed and famine brought an end to the glorious Mayan communities.

21

FEATHERED SERPENT: EARLY INDIAN GOD

THE high Central Valley of Mexico was the cradle of another great Mexican Indian culture. Ringed by a wall of imposing mountains, the fertile valley held a large salt lake, Texcoco, where the Aztecs later built their capital. But long before the Aztecs wandered into Central Mexico, an Indian city named Teotihuacán (TEH-*oh-tee-wah-kahn*) thrived and then was deserted here.

The young Mexicans in this picture have come to see the wonders of this city that was probably built in the early years of the Christian era. The story of the people who built it is lost in the mists of time. All we know is that they left some pyramids as great as those found in Egypt, and that their god was the same plumed serpent found in later Mayan and Aztec carvings. The ruins of Teotihuacán are only thirty-five miles northeast of Mexico City. It is said that Montezuma (*mon-teh-*zoo*-mah*), the Aztec king, was so awed by these majestic and deserted pyramids that he used to come here to make sacrifices to the old gods. Visitors today marvel at the vanished race who produced them.

The strikingly fierce carved head glowering above the children is Quetzalcoatl, the plumed serpent. He represented both the earth and sky united in one godlike being. It was Quetzalcoatl who supposedly brought the arts of civilization to the Indians, and they had many legends about him. One of these told that the god made a prophecy to his people before leaving them. He promised to return in a certain year from across the sea. Then he sailed away to the east on a raft of coiled serpents.

The arrival of Cortés, bearded and white skinned, from that same sea to the east, struck fear into the heart of Montezuma. Here was an ancient prophecy fulfilled, and the Aztec king had no alternative but to open his doors to the white god and make him welcome.

22

LAUNCHES AT XOCHIMILCO: SUNDAY AFTERNOON EXCURSION

THE floating gardens at Xochimilco (*soh-chee*-MEEL-*koh*) are a favorite recreation spot outside Mexico City. They are the last remnants of the fabled floating gardens of the Aztec princes, and we can see why, when the Spaniards had their first amazed sight of the Aztec capital, they described it as the "Venice of the New World." At Xochimilco the ancient canals still wind between little islands, each of which is massed with flowers. But actually the gardens no longer float. Originally the Indians had built large rafts covered with a thin layer of dirt where they planted their vegetables and flowers. Now the old rafts are firmly anchored to the mud, and tall poplars grow along the canals.

All of the boats are decked with flowers, and even their names are flowery and romantic. Aztec boatmen pole them through the green water, and they call out to one another in their mysterious old language. The boats are furnished with chairs and tables, and out on the canals there are other boats that sell food and drinks and fresh flowers. Families come to picnic on the water on Sundays and young couples come to court. Where there are Mexicans there is bound to be music, so some of the launches carry small orchestras. But even though Xochimilco is crowded with tourists, there is a languid beauty in the Place of Flowers, and its color and fragrance linger in the memory of the delighted visitor.

A boatload of flowers adds a note of color to the canals of Xochimilco.

25

GRASSHOPPER HILL: OVERLOOKING MEXICO CITY

MODERN skyscrapers rise from the old lake bed where Montezuma's proud city once stood. From the heights of Chapultepec (*chah-pool-teh-*PECK), the Aztec name for Grasshopper Hill, the view of Mexico City is impressive. Here, under ancient trees said to have been planted by the Aztec king himself, gay crowds of Mexicans throng to Chapultepec to enjoy the shaded walks, band concerts, horseback riding and the old castle that is now a museum.

In this picture we are on the terrace of the castle, a romantic spot colored by the historic events that took place here. Once an Aztec temple loomed above the city at the crest of this hill. In 1783 Chapultepec Castle was built by a Spanish viceroy for his red-haired bride. After the Wars of Independence in the early nineteenth century the building became the National Military Academy.

During the Mexican-American War in 1847 this hilltop was valiantly defended against the United States soldiers by students of the Academy. Six of the Boy Heroes have been immortalized by a monument

In the midst of modern civilization the patient Indian retains his timeless quality.

at the base of the rocky hill. When they were no longer able to hold the hill against advancing forces, the six boys, with true Latin bravura, wrapped themselves in Mexican flags and leapt to their death from the parapet. But the castle is best known as the home of Mexico's last Emperor — Maximilian — and his Empress, Carlotta.

MAXIMILIAN'S CARRIAGE: INSIDE CHAPULTEPEC CASTLE

IT IS hard to believe that this elegant carriage once rolled grandly down the streets of Mexico City bearing an Emperor and Empress. The chapter of Mexican history dealing with Maximilian and Carlotta is short, tragic and almost like a work of fiction. In 1864 Mexico's internal affairs were so chaotic that Napoleon III of France was able to intervene and send Maximilian of Austria to govern, supposedly at Mexico's request.

This well-meaning Hapsburg prince and his wife spent three years in Mexico, but without the support of French arms their reign was doomed. They beautified Mexico City—both of them were cultivated people of taste. And they united the country—inadvertently. To all classes and parties the Emperor was a hated foreigner and they had to oppose him and be free once again. Poor Carlotta lost her mind when it became certain that Maximilian would be overthrown. He died before a firing squad—bravely, as befitted an Emperor—crying "¡Viva Mexico!"

The man who succeeded Maximilian was a full-blooded Indian named Benito Juárez. He was responsible for the Reform Movement (known as *La Reforma*) after which Maximilian's beautiful boulevard in Mexico City was later named. Juárez tried to correct the economic inequalities that existed in his country by redistributing the wealth concentrated in a few hands and spreading it among the dispossessed masses.

As far back as 1625 a visitor to Mexico City was struck with the lavish coaches used by the Spanish inhabitants. He wrote, "In Mexico there are four things fair, the women, the apparel, the horses and the streets. But to this I may add the beauty of some of the coaches of the gentry, for they spare no silver, nor gold, nor precious stones, nor cloth of gold nor the best silks of China to enrich them." Maximilian's coach was certainly in this tradition! But after the Emperor was executed, Juárez came to Mexico City to take over the government. He rode to the National Palace in a plain black carriage. The days of pomp and circumstance were over.

PASEO DE LA REFORMA: MEXICO CITY'S HANDSOME BOULEVARD

ALTHOUGH Mexico City is in the Torrid Zone, its altitude —7400 feet above sea level —gives it a climate of perpetual springtime. All year round the city is brightened with the fresh green of trees and grass and the vivid hues of flowers. The Paseo de la Reforma (*pah-*SEH*-oh deh lah reh-*FOR*-mah*), which we see here, is one of the most beautiful avenues in the world. In 1866, when Maximilian and Carlotta went to live in Chapultepec Castle, the Empress had the avenue landscaped like a long narrow park. It is punctuated with *glorietas,* little circular gardens, each surrounding a statue or monument. The legend is that this devoted wife wanted to watch her husband's pleasant progress as his coach rolled down the boulevard from the Castle where they lived to the National Palace where he had his offices.

Mexico City has changed from the elegant French-style capital that it was in those days. Smart hotels and glass-walled office buildings shoulder the small but ornate mansions of another era. Because the city is built on the bed of an old lake, its subsoil is spongy and acts as a shock-absorber in times of earthquakes. Mexico City's new skyscrapers are built on pylons that "float" them in the soft ground or rest on the rock below. The tall buildings sparkle boldly above the city, defying the two famous volcanoes, Popocatépetl and Iztaccihuatl, that tower in the distance.

The power and the energy of present-day Mexico are celebrated in its art and architecture.

30

THE CATHEDRAL OF MEXICO CITY: LARGEST IN THE AMERICAS

THE great main square of Mexico City was once the center of the royal Aztec capital. When Cortés and the Spaniards took it over, they rebuilt the city according to Spanish taste, and this center became a plaza. The holiest of the Aztec temples stood where the Cathedral is now. It had been the scene of incredibly bloody human sacrifices, and the Spaniards lost little time in tearing it down and erecting a church in its place. The thousands of Indians whom they hoped to convert believed that the site itself was holy, and it was not too difficult to wean them from their old gods and lead them to the new religion.

In 1573, the small church was torn down and work was begun on the present imposing cathedral. It was not completed until 1813, and consequently it is made up of the architectural styles of many periods. Many archaeologists believe that the Cathedral's foundation is made of debris from the ruined Aztec temple that stood on this site. The famous Aztec calendar stone was found here when excavations were made to enlarge the Cathedral.

On another side of The Plaza of the Constitution, or the Zócalo (so-*kah-loh*), the National Palace stands, a solid block-square building. This is where Montezuma's fabulous palace dazzled the eyes of Cortés. After Cortés had repaid Montezuma's hospitality by conquering him and his people, he rebuilt the palace as a kind of fortress. Only a small part of the original Cortés building still remains, but inside the palace as it stands today you can see the history of Mexico depicted in the brilliant frescoes of Diego Rivera (DYAY-*go ree*-VAY-*rah*), the great modern Mexican artist.

The Mexican bell of independence hangs over the center door, and the President of the Republic rings it every September 16th. The plaza is jammed then with excited Mexicans, and the President steps out on a balcony and shouts the famous "*grito*" (GREE-*toh*) or cry, "¡Viva Mexico!" with which Mexican independence was heralded in 1810.

33

INDIAN DANCERS: FESTIVAL OUTSIDE THE CATHEDRAL

NOW we have moved up close to the great Cathedral, and are standing in the paved area that separates it from the street. During the Spanish rule this Cathedral was the place of worship for the wealthy colonials. Splendid masses were held inside, and magnificent processions wound their stately way into the streets. But since the great reforms of a hundred years ago, this Cathedral has become the church for all classes, and the Indians are particularly in evidence.

In the sixteenth century, when the missionaries first converted thousands of the Aztecs to Christianity, they were aware of the Indians' love of singing and dancing. The priests adapted Aztec war dances to religious ceremonials in which saints fought against devils. They encouraged the Indians to retain their colorful *fiestas*, but substituted Christian holidays and saints for pagan celebrations and idols. These brilliantly colorful rituals permitted the Indians to retain a sense of their own identity while joining forces spiritually with the Spaniards. In this way the Indians had something to hold them together when they became a subjugated people.

These dancers performing in the courtyard of the Cathedral are not profaning it. Their primitive dances and music and their vividly colored costumes go back to pagan times, but the religious spirit that animates them today is Christian.

34

CHARRO EXHIBITION: THE ART OF HORSEMANSHIP

ONE of the favorite recreations in Mexico is horseback riding and the reason for its popularity is bound up with the country's history. Shortly after Cortés came to Mexico he wrote back to Spain, "After God, our only security was the horses." As long as the Spaniards could keep their horses exclusively, they had a dramatic symbol of their superiority over the Indian who walked on foot. So Indians were not permitted to own horses or to ride them. To be a *"caballero"* (*kah-bah-*LYEH-*roh*), or horseman, was also to be a gentleman—the word means both in Spanish.

Naturally, as soon as they could, the Indian and part-Indian ranchers began to raise horses. Well-to-do ranchers lavished money on fancy saddles, bridles and elaborate riding costumes, and they developed a remarkable repertoire of stunts on horseback. These men were called *"charros"* (CHAR-*rohs*). The *charro* is a national figure today and, after the bullfighter, this equestrian acrobat is probably the most admired sportsman in Mexico. The women riders are called *charras*, and we see a group of them here at a riding club in Mexico City. They dress in the long, full-skirted national costume and wear broad-brimmed sombreros. Thus encumbered, they ride sidesaddle, but even so some of them are able to perform with the *charros* in their most daring stunts, including bullfighting on horseback.

This daredevil charro will pursue the bull on horseback and toss him to the ground while the crowd goes wild.

MEXICAN
BULLFIGHT:
BRAVERY IN
THE AFTERNOON

THE most popular national sport is the *corrida* (kor-REE-dah), or bullfight. However unpunctual nearly everything else is in Mexico, on Sunday afternoon *promptly* at four o'clock the bullfight begins. It is a brilliant and barbaric spectacle, with the matadors and their helpers marching into the sand-covered arena in their splendid costumes. The band blares, the fans go wild, and the old ritual begins. Bullfighting was brought to Mexico by the Spaniards, and its appeal was instantaneous. Nearly every town has a *corrida* of some sort on *fiesta* days. But Mexico City has the finest bull ring, the Plaza Mexico, and it attracts the best matadors in the world.

The ring has seats in the sun and in the shade. The sun section, called *Sol* (*sohl*), has the cheaper seats. Places in the *Sombra* (SOHM-*brah*), or shade section, cost more than twice as much. The real fans occupy the sunny seats, and cushions, pop bottles, and sometimes wooden parts of the bleachers get hurled into the ring when these critics are displeased with the action. When the matador has completed an exceptionally

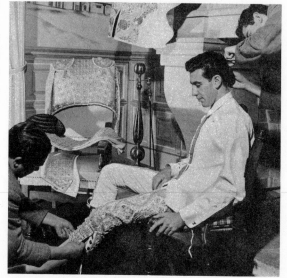

The bullfighter's costume is showy and protective. His "suit of lights" weighs eighteen pounds, and the braid of hair guards the base of his skull.

brave or beautiful pass, the band strikes up a song called "La Diana," a cheer set to music. In this picture the matador is executing the graceful passes with his big cape that will enable him to judge the speed and temper of his four-legged opponent. Later, when it is time for the kill, the matador will use a small red cape and his sword. We will not stay for the bloody finale.

UNIVERSITY CITY: MODERN EDUCATIONAL CENTER

THE ultramodern campus that we see in this picture is a far cry from the ivy-covered buildings that typify most United States universities. Yet the National University of Mexico was chartered in 1551—nearly a hundred years earlier than Harvard, and it is the oldest university in the New World. Until 1952, when this campus was completed, the university was housed in a scattered group of monasteries, convents and colonial mansions throughout Mexico City. In 1950 President Alemán (*ah-leh*-MAHN) appropriated funds for a new university plant, and it was built at a cost of about fifty million dollars.

Employing a staff of a hundred and fifty architects, and the best painters and sculptors in a country noted for its artists, Alemán had the university built on the broad acreage of the lava fields on the city's outskirts. The tall building in the background is the handsome library—one of the best examples of modern Mexican architecture. It was designed practically without windows so that the unbroken walls inside would hold the maximum amount of bookshelves, and the outside walls could be used for vast mosaic murals. They are the work of the Mexican artist and architect Juan O'Gorman, and on them he has pictured the story of Mexican culture from pre-conquest to modern times.

University City is aptly named. There are about thirty thousand students enrolled, and the campus includes a science building, a stadium for one hundred thousand people, a liberal arts building one-quarter of a mile long, a nuclear physics and a cosmic ray laboratory, a giant swimming pool, and schools of medicine and dentistry. The university granted nearly forty thousand degrees during the three centuries of colonial rule. But in those days education in Mexico was only for the aristocrats. Today popular education is one of the country's great aims, and many of her young people have as their goal the bright buildings of University City.

41

WASHERWOMAN
AT TAXCO:
PRIMITIVE
LAUNDRY

THERE are many Mexicos today, for the country is in transition—a primitive land in the process of becoming modernized. So while we see some young people dressed in collegiate styles against the background of the modern university, we also find girls like this one still washing clothes at the village cistern.

Mexican women have made an art of what would seem to us a difficult and unpleasant task. Skillfully, rhythmically, without a wasted motion, they soak the clothes first, soap them lavishly, pound them against the rocks, rinse, soap and rinse again. While the dirt is scrubbed out of the clothes, and the women's hands move with grace and economy, their tongues are going a mile a minute, and much of the village dirt also comes out over the wash.

Here in Taxco (TAHSS-*koh*) we see one of the most picturesque towns in all Mexico. But the quaint charm of this and other villages has its drawbacks, as responsible Mexicans are only too well aware, and they are trying to modernize the country as rapidly as they can. One of the biggest problems the country has to face is dramatized in this picture. Water, and particularly good drinking water, is in short supply. Mexico's death rate because of diseases caused by polluted water is sixty times higher than ours. Consequently, when they can, Mexicans buy bottled drinks, and American soft drinks have nearly become the "wine of the land."

It is in the little towns of the central highlands that the water shortage is most severe. A family's most cherished possession is the tin pail used for carrying the precious water from a public fountain. Aside from the risk of serious illness, the families who live in waterless houses have the problem of keeping clean. Most Taxco houses have water piped into them now, but in smaller villages, once darkness has fallen, bathers make a stealthy trip to the public fountain and take a quick shower there while their neighbors sleep.

42

TOWN PLAZA: MEMENTO OF SPAIN

THERE are two kinds of towns in Mexico—the primitive Indian settlements of adobe huts, and those little replicas of Spain built by Spanish colonizers in the years when they ruled Mexico. Most towns of any size or charm bear the Spanish imprint, and in Taxco we see one of the pleasant plazas typical of hundreds of colonial Mexican towns. These little squares were copied from remembered cities in Spain, and around the green and shady oasis the municipal buildings and church are grouped.

The plaza is the focal point of every Mexican town. Originally it was a cobbled square used for military drills and parades, and it was from these squares that the Spaniards dominated the surrounding countryside and smaller Indian villages. In the nineteenth century Maximilian and Carlotta, who loved beautiful gardens, ordered trees and flowers planted in all the plazas.

In Taxco, giant laurels shade the little plaza where band concerts are held several times a week. On other evenings wandering marimba players, hammering their primitive xylophones, make music under the trees while people parade along the plaza walks. Young men flirt with young women, and agile Mexican children dart in and out of the crowds vending shoelaces, chewing gum and assorted trifles. It is then, in the cool hours of darkness, that the plaza truly becomes the pulsing heart of a Mexican town.

"The Chiclét Kid" is a common sight in this country where chewing gum originated.

45

STROLLING ORCHESTRA: MEXICAN SERENADE

MEXICO is a land of music and the Latin rhythms of her songs are heard everywhere. One of the most popular sources of melody is the strolling folk orchestra known as the *mariachi* (*mah-RYAH-chee*). There are anywhere from three to a dozen men in the group, and their instruments are predominantly stringed. These little orchestras were great favorites with Maximilian, and while he was emperor they were often hired to play at wedding parties in the homes of his French courtiers. It is believed that the bands were then first called *mariachis* from the French word for wedding—*mariage* (*mah-RYAHZH*).

In the markets and plazas of villages and towns the gay tunes of the *mariachis* are an ever-present accompaniment to the activity. The songs grow louder as the band approaches and fade away as the musicians stroll off into the distance. They will stop and play for anyone who offers to pay them, and often they are hired to play for a special *fiesta* or serenade. In Mexico City the *mariachis* have achieved real professional standing, and there they perform on radio programs, in movies and for

In Paracho the making of fine guitars is a family art. This boy began when he was six and is now an expert.

recording companies. Originally the village bands were given their instruments by the government and excused from the other communal work of the village in return for furnishing music. The catch was that a band that did not practice could be thrown in jail. Today the *mariachi* players are on their own, and they find that practice not only makes perfect— it makes pesos as well.

46

VIEW OF
TAXCO:
CITY OF SILVER

THE world's supply of silver was doubled in the period from the seventeenth to the nineteenth centuries, and this new flood of precious metal flowed from the silver mines of Mexico. It made men rich, and they in turn beautified the towns that were responsible for their wealth. José de la Borda (*hoh-*SEH *deh lah* BOHR-*dah*) was riding a horse on this hillside in Taxco when the animal's hoof was trapped in a soft spot on the rock. The soft ore turned out to be an outcropping of a vein of silver—the fabled San Carlos lode on which Borda's fortune was founded.

Wishing to show his gratitude to the town, the silver king built the rose-colored Church of Santa Prisca (SAHN-*tah* PREESS-*kah*), whose towers we see here. He poured ten million pesos into its construction and then said grandly, "God gives to Borda and Borda gives to God." When he later lost his money, the archbishop permitted him to take back a diamond-studded gold chalice which had been part of his gift. With that stake he recouped his fortune and, presumably, continued his philanthropies.

Taxco's beauty is protected, for it is considered a national monument, and no building is permitted here without the approval of federal architects. The narrow streets are cobbled, as they were in colonial days, and they wind steeply between whitewashed houses with red tile roofs. Follow any one of them, and you are bound to find yourself in a charming and picturesque spot. Here, branching off from the little plaza near the church, are some of Taxco's shops where the silver flow has been reversed—today it is tourist silver that pours into Taxco.

COPPER
VENDOR:
LOW-PRESSURE
SALESMAN

THIS young man in the Taxco market is watching the shop —but just barely. He is immersed in a comic book, trusting to the copper gleam of the hand-made pots to attract customers. If that fails he has a sideline in walnuts.

Taxco has some highly skilled tinsmiths, too, who make the stylized tin masks, mirror frames, cigarette boxes and candelabra so dear to the hearts (and so easy on the pocketbooks) of many tourists. But the town's most famous artisans are the silversmiths. In 1930 an American named William Spratling settled in Taxco, and he is responsible for reviving the art of working in silver, an art that had flourished in this silver town many years ago. The feeling for decoration and the skill necessary to produce good folk art have been present in Mexico since long before the conquest. Spratling inspired and encouraged the people to make beautiful silver pieces once again.

There is a story—which may or may not be true—that the representative of a large American company came to one of the Taxco silversmiths and wanted to place an order with him for several hundred dozen brooches, all of the same design. The man had been charging $2.50 for a brooch. "But for two hundred dozen, señor, the price will have to be $3.50 each." In vain the American tried to explain that they should be cheaper in such large lots. "No, no, señor," the silversmith insisted. "I must charge more when I make so many. You see, I will be so *bored* making them all the same!"

You can visit some of the silver mines near Taxco by car or on horseback. There are dirt roads winding through the hills around the town and going up into the mountains. This is wonderful country to explore on horseback, and who knows, you may have the same sort of lucky accident that Borda, the silver king, had.

MARKET IN CUERNAVACA: CARNIVAL FOR SHOPPERS

HALFWAY between Taxco and Mexico City is Cuernavaca (*kwair-nah-*VAH-*kah*), a semitropical town that is a favorite weekend retreat for wealthy residents of the capital. Its altitude is almost three thousand feet lower than Mexico City's, and its gentler atmosphere is a relief from the strain of living seven thousand feet above sea level. Cuernavaca's elaborate homes, set amidst lush gardens, are a vivid contrast to the poorer Indian section of the city. The extremes of wealth and poverty, the modern and the primitive, are as typical of Mexico as her high mountains and deep valleys.

Though Cuernavaca has some of the most marvelous shops for tourists in the entire country, its outdoor market is even more interesting to visit. In this picture we see one of the larger market streets—a fairly grand one by the standards of smaller towns. In most village markets the Indians come in from the surrounding country, and their wares are spread out on the ground or on crude boxes or tables. Every village market has its own local specialty. Some are known for their pottery, some for their serapes, some for leather goods and some for their tin or metalwork. Fruits, vegetables and those Mexican staples, beans and corn, are also on hand. The smells of the market are a compound of highly spiced foods, fruits, leather and humanity. For tourists the markets are a novel experience. Where in the wide world could you buy a decorative clay jug, made by hand, for only a dime?

The rhythmic slap-slapping of the tortilla makers is a familiar sound in the market. These corn cakes are the Mexicans' bread.

VALLEY OF
PUEBLA:
TWO-PASSENGER
BURRO

THE high valley of Puebla (PWEH-*blah*), some eighty miles from Mexico City, was once the domain of the god Quetzalcoatl. Cortés, on his march from the sea to the Aztec capital, swept through this valley destroying hundreds of pyramid temples on his way—there is said to have been a temple for every day of the year. The Spaniards then built Christian churches on top of each of the demolished temples, and their tile domes gleam in the unusually clear air of the valley.

In this picture we see a barefoot Mexican father and his little boy astride the family burro. Their valley is ringed with four volcanoes, two of them the famous twins—Popocatépetl and Iztaccihuatl. When Cortés marched this way, his route lay through the pass between the two volcanoes. His supply of gunpowder was exhausted after his assault on the natives of the valley, and the ingenious conqueror had one of his men lowered into the crater of Popocatépetl to dig out some sulphur for more powder.

Though the influence of Spain is seen in the buildings, pottery and fine tiles made in this section of the country, the rural people have remained distinctly Mexican. The father and son seen here are typical, with their bare feet and broad-brimmed sombreros. These hats, woven by hand of palm leaves, are worn by Mexican men—and occasionally by women, too—as a shield from the sun. Each section of Mexico makes its sombreros differently. Some have wider brims, others have taller crowns; in some places the men prefer sombreros trimmed with colored wool, feathers or bands of plaited leather. *Charros* wear felt sombreros that more closely resemble the original Spanish article. But though the hats may vary from district to district, the brown face beneath the brim is always proudly Mexican.

54

CHURCH INTERIOR: ALTAR IN THE CITY OF THE ANGELS

IN PUEBLA, the fourth largest city of the Republic, the Spaniards left some of the most magnificent buildings in the New World. The elaborate architecture of many Mexican churches has a spun-sugar ornateness that goes beyond the wildest dreams of a fancy pastry chef, but occasionally the style is handled so well that we are dazzled by the color and intricate workmanship. That is true of the Church of San Francisco (St. Francis), which we see here. This church is of special interest because of its small image of Our Lady of Health which Cortés is said to have brought from Spain.

But Puebla is famous throughout Mexico for another lady—one of the most dearly beloved in the entire country. She is the *China Poblana* (CHEE-*nah poh*-BLAH-*nah*), or Puebla China-girl, a semilegendary Chinese princess who was captured by pirates and sold to a merchant of Puebla. Converted to Christianity, the princess put aside her Oriental finery and dressed instead in a plain red flannel skirt and an embroidered white cotton blouse. Her goodness, grace and charity earned her the love of the townspeople, and in her memory the women adopted her costume. The *china poblana*, with elaborate embellishments, has now become the national costume and, naturally, Puebla sells the prettiest ones in all Mexico.

The china poblana is the colorful national costume that sets off the flashing beauty of Mexican girls.

ACAPULCO: SEASIDE PARADISE

THIS glittering resort town on its own blue curve of bay is a little North American Riviera. Whatever Mexican character it once had has been almost wholly obliterated by its more than one hundred and fifty hotels, its modern airport and its throngs of international vacationers. True, there are a little plaza, a market and red-tiled roofs in the town behind the hotels. But the overwhelming impression you have of Acapulco is of blue sky and water and golden beaches, with luxury hotels built into the surrounding hills. Mexico has enjoyed an enormous boom since World War II. She now can put up many more of her guests in first-class accommodations, and most of her own people are also living better than they ever did before.

Acapulco is not just a foreigners' resort. It is a popular vacation spot for the inhabitants of Mexico City, who feel the need for coming down from that high altitude every once in a while. Acapulco, at sea level, and with fishing, swimming and water sports that are unavailable up on the central plateau, is the ideal spot. In case you tire of one beach there are about half a dozen, each for a different time of day, and one more beautiful than the other. If your pulse still needs quickening, you can drive to a rocky cliff called La Quebrada (*lah keh*-BRAH-*dah*). Down at its foot the warm sea swirls and eddies around the rocks. On the cliff, copper-skinned native boys perform the immemorial stunt of diving for coins into the dangerous waters sixty feet below. It is a sight that would have pleased their tough old Aztec ancestors.

Traces have been found, a few miles from Acapulco, of an Aztec fishing village. It is believed that Indian runners took the fresh catch and ran from the coast up through the mountain passes to Tenochtitlán, the Aztec capital, arriving before the fish spoiled. It was proved to be possible when some Indian runners tried it during President Alemán's administration. They arrived in Mexico City slightly winded, but the fish, wrapped in wet leaves, were fresher than the runners.

LAKE PATZCUARO: FISHING WITH A BUTTERFLY NET

ABOUT two hundred miles due west of Mexico City is Lake Pátzcuaro (PAHTS-*kwah-roh*), still and blue in the clear air at 6700 feet above sea level. The town of Pátzcuaro (which means Place of Delights) is on its hilly shores, and the picturesque fishing village of Janitzio (*hah-*NEETS-*yoh*) is on a green island in the lake. The fishermen of Janitzio are a proud group. Their skill is legendary, and everywhere on the small island you can see their nets drying or being woven or mended. The unusual butterfly nets, which are traditional with these people, keep men, women and children busy. After a month's use the net needs to be repaired; after three months it is completely worn out and a new one must be made. If the Indians could buy a stronger sort of thread—nylon, for example—their nets would probably last ten times as long. But nylon has not yet put in an appearance at Pátzcuaro.

The great delicacy for which these fine nets are especially constructed is a small, silvery, almost transparent lake fish. In the winter months the people of the villages scattered around the lake have another wonderful sport—wild duck hunting. They wait until a flock of ducks has settled on the water. Then hundreds of canoes are paddled out from shore, closing in on the ducks from all directions. When the ducks flap up into the air, the hunters harpoon them with skillfully thrown spears. Later they all feast on wild duck, unspoiled by buckshot. Maybe their way is better!

The little island of Janitzio is crowned by a heroic statue of Morelos, the martyred patriot-priest.

61

LOCAL FIESTA: DANCE OF THE LITTLE OLD MEN

ONE of the most distinctive folk dances of Mexico is performed in the region around Lake Pátzcuaro. It is known as *Los Viejitos* (*lohs vyeh-*HEE*-tohs*), the Little Old Men. Mexican speech is peppered with diminutives—the *ito* ending, which means "little," is added to many words to indicate affection as well as smallness. The Mexicans themselves are smaller than the average in other Western countries due to the nutritional deficiencies in their diet over a long period. Perhaps because of this, they have a fondness for tiny things and have become skilled at making miniature carvings, diminutive toys and figures that fit into a nutshell. And they have emphasized their small size in the name of this dance.

The performers are usually agile young men dressed in white cotton suits and heavy shoes, and wearing masks of grotesquely old faces. They carry canes and are apparently stooped with age. At the beginning of

These bird-men are the daring Pole Dancers, who plummet earthward on their ropes in re-enactment of an Aztec rite.

the dance the *Viejitos* shamble around, decrepit and feeble. Suddenly the music becomes gay, and the hunchbacked oldsters break into a virile and spirited dance, their feet stamping out an intricate rhythm. Without missing a beat, the dancers clown and shove one another roughly, competing in the complicated figures and horseplay that are part of the dance. This performance has been handed down from the times before the conquest and its comedy still gets laughs today.

NATIVE DUGOUTS: PATZCUARO'S PRIMITIVE CRAFT

WHEN we look at this picture we can see that the twentieth century has scarcely reached these people. The Indians around Lake Pátzcuaro are Tarascans (*tah-*RAH*-skans*), one of the few groups who proudly claim never to have been conquered by the Aztecs. Those Tarascans who lived on the island of Janitzio had kept their old civilization almost unchanged, and they continued to speak Tarascan rather than Spanish, so untouched were they by the world beyond their gleaming lake.

Then in 1922 one of the young men of the island went to live in the town of Pátzcuaro, where he worked for a Mexican family. A government official offered the boy two pesos a day if he would go back to his island and persuade his people to make friendly contact with their mainland neighbors. This was accomplished and now the islanders speak Spanish, traffic with visitors and pick up a few pesos on occasion in return for ferrying people around the lake in their old dugouts.

According to local legend one of these hand-hewn dugouts was found floating on Lake Pátzcuaro four hundred years ago. The Indian who discovered it reported that its sole occupant was a miraculous image of Our Lady of Health. This image, a very fragile one made of cornstalk paste, is now enshrined in one of Pátzcuaro's churches. It may be that Bishop Quiroga (*kee-*ROH*-gah*), who came here in 1540 to help the natives, asked them to make the image for their new church. The Bishop was greatly loved by these proud people. He taught them crafts, and encouraged and organized them in the production of copper utensils, beautiful pottery, and painted lacquer ware for which this region is still famous.

In this scene you can see the Indians' precious cornfield. Even on the shores of a lake where fish are plentiful, corn—the Indians' chief food— is a necessary crop. It is to them what rice is to Asiatics.

TARASCAN INDIANS: BARTERING THEIR WARES

IN ISOLATED and primitive communities like those around Lake Pátzcuaro, the Indians still exchange their products instead of selling them. Here in Erongarícuaro (*eh-rohn-gah-*REE-*kwah-roh*), a tiny village with a long name, the Tarascans have a fascinating Sunday market where they come to barter as they have done for centuries. Each village in this region specializes in one particular craft, originally taught to its inhabitants by the good Bishop Quiroga. When Sunday comes, those who have made baskets may trade them for fish or corn or a bag woven by a woman of another village.

Looking at these women, you would never guess that on at least one occasion their lives have been touched with romance and drama. The Tarascans have a unique marriage custom. In Mexico, where the proprieties are carefully observed, a young man must ask for the hand of his bride. But among the Tarascans it is customary for the would-be groom to kidnap a girl, and afterwards get her parents' consent for the wedding. Usually the bride is stolen on a Sunday morning as she walks home from church with the other women of the family. She struggles and fights her abductor and the Sunday stillness is broken by her outraged shouts—all this in spite of the fact that the girl has consented in advance to being stolen!

If the boy can get his captive bride to an uncle's house before her male relatives are able to catch them, he is permitted to hide her there. Then he can negotiate with the girl's parents from a position of strength, and since no one else will marry her once she has been stolen, a marriage is eventually arranged. These women probably enjoy reminiscing about their romantic weddings as they go about the more mundane business of wives and mothers.

ADOBE MAKER:
MEXICAN BRICKS
DRY IN THE SUN

THE village men make a community enterprise of brickmaking, and we can see them at work on the outskirts of many Mexican towns. The red clay soil may not yield much in the way of food, but it does give the people an ideal material for shelter. Better than trees which would have to be cut down, or stone which would have to be quarried, here is a building material right at hand, without even the problem of transportation. Furthermore it is absolutely free.

The men of the village dig up the soil and mix it with water and straw. The adobe maker we see here is in luck. His village is near one of the few Mexican rivers, so his water supply is convenient and doesn't have to be hauled in buckets. Square wooden molds are filled with the muddy mixture and set out to dry in the hot sun. We can get some idea of how extensively adobe is used when we realize that there are more than two million houses made of these bricks, out of a total of around five million dwellings in Mexico. Some of these buildings are over a hundred years old, and are still in good condition.

We can see in this picture that the village youngsters must find the whole procedure fascinating. What small boy wouldn't love an opportunity to make mud pies on so large a scale? This young fellow is probably itching to get his hands on Daddy's adobe and when the time comes, he will be proud to join in the men's work of the village.

These children live in a thatched hut, yet their dresses are hand embroidered. Folk art beautifies everyday objects.

69

THE MAGUEY:
PLANT OF A
HUNDRED USES

THE fleshy-leaved maguey (*mah*-GAY), known to us as the century plant, is a common sight along the roads and in the fields of Mexico. And no wonder! This one plant supplies the Mexicans' most popular liquor, pins, nails, paper, soap, fibers for thread or rope, firewood, shoes and thatching for houses—just to give you some idea of its versatility. It is cultivated and grown in abundance, but its popularity is due primarily to the fact that pulque (POOL-*keh*), the most widely used intoxicant in Mexico, is made from the maguey's fermented juice.

In central Mexico there are enormous pulque haciendas (*ah*-SYEHN-*dahs*), plantations largely devoted to the cultivation of maguey and the manufacture and marketing of pulque. The Indians who live and work on the haciendas in almost feudal servitude are paid part of their wages in pulque. The drink has about the same alcoholic content as beer, and is a gray, thick, slightly sweet liquid which, fortunately, has considerable nutritional value. In the poorer classes even children drink pulque to supplement their meager diets. But some of the Mexican men consume quarts of pulque each day, and they go about in a slightly alcoholic stupor from mid-afternoon on.

On the great pulque haciendas there are skilled workers who suck the juice from the maguey by means of a long gourd. The barrels of sap are then brought to the brewery, where the master pulque-maker mixes it with a batch of specially fermented juice and pours it into vats. His process is a secret, and the pouring is a solemn ritual attended by workers who reverently remove their hats and chant an ancient prayer. Their Indian ancestors must have observed similar rites, for pulque was a ceremonial drink of the Toltecs and Aztecs. The versatile maguey has been cultivated for more than a thousand years and its role in Mexican life is so important that the plant is known as the people's "good provider."

WALKING TO MARKET: FAMILY OUTING

IN THE region around Tlaxcala (*tlah*-SKAH-*lah*), which we see here, the great pulque haciendas are giving way to the communal farm villages of the poor that resulted from the land reforms of this century. Although progress is being made in Mexico, there are some things that seem never to change, and one of them is the tradition of market day. Before the white man came to Mexico, the mountainous country and the lack of transportation made local trading centers vitally important. The Indians had to carry their own goods to market and they walked, heavily burdened, along rough trails.

Today many Mexicans still walk to market, though some have burros, horses and even trucks. This weekly event is the only social life available to the rural people, and it breaks the monotony of their days of poverty and toil. During the week a family's scant leisure may be spent in making a few clay jugs, weaving a woolen serape or some straw mats, growing a few extra fruits or vegetables. Then on market day these objects, made with neither overhead nor transportation costs, can be sold for the few pesos that mean the difference between bare subsistence and a little extra. Furthermore, the market is more fun if you have something to sell.

In the first clear light of a Mexican morning, people from the outlying country start the market-day journey. Families are dressed in their best and cleanest clothes, and a carnival atmosphere prevails. The market draws the bright throng to it like a magnet, and the changeless Indian need to mingle in a warm and colorful crowd is satisfied.

A Mexican bus careens along the dusty road, overflowing with merry passengers.

BOY WEAVING:
YOUNG HANDS,
OLD SKILL

WE HAVE traveled down south of the girdle of mountains and volcanoes that bands central Mexico and are now in the remote valley of Oaxaca (*wah*-HAH-*kah*). Here the hills are blue and purple in the distance. The colonial city of Oaxaca has a sturdy beauty—its houses are built like fortresses to withstand the earthquakes in this region, and many of them are made of a dull green stone that takes on a gemlike luster in the rain.

Of all the sections of Mexico, Oaxaca is the most outstanding for its handicrafts. Leather goods, flowered pottery and hand-woven textiles are superb, and, perhaps as relaxation from their more serious labors, the artisans here turn out delightful toys, too. Straw horses and burros, painted clay dolls and angels, gay little whistles and bells all are to be found in the markets here as well as the fine saddles, dinner sets, blankets and *rebozos* for which Oaxaca is renowned.

The boy in our picture is industriously weaving a long strip of fine woolen fabric for a *rebozo*. The rich red color of the dye is a specialty of Oaxaca, too. It is called cochineal (*koch-ih*-NEEL), and it is made from the dried bodies of a kind of tiny insect that thrives in Oaxaca. This red dye is an important export product. *Rebozos* are worn and made all over Mexico, but some of the finest ones are made here. The Spanish women brought the mantilla to Mexico, and the Indians adapted it to suit their own purposes. Primarily this long scarflike cloth is used as a head covering when a woman enters a church. But it is also worn wrapped around her shoulders for a coat, slung on her back as a baby-carrier, doubled over and filled with fruits and vegetables as if it were a basket. When an Indian woman sleeps, her *rebozo* is her cover. When she carries water from the fountain, the *rebozo* is folded like a cushion under the heavy jar on top of her head. In short, the strip of cloth this boy is weaving is equivalent to a closetful of clothes and accessories.

74

MARKET DAY:
FESTIVE
OCCASION

ONE of the liveliest and most colorful markets in Mexico is in the little village of Tlacolula (*tlah-koh-*LOO-*lah*), not far from Oaxaca. Here, on Sundays, the Indians from the surrounding mountain villages come bearing a fascinating assortment of goods and produce to sell. The sprawling market place is really as orderly as a department store. Although there are few stalls at Tlacolula and most of the wares are spread out on the ground, custom has dictated that vendors of each type of merchandise occupy certain sections, and there is an unspoken agreement giving each person a right to the same location week after week.

The Indians have an innate feeling for color and form, and they arrange their displays artistically. From a distance the market looks like a work of art with bright splashes of color, mounds of pottery, vivid lengths of cloth and patterned arrangements of vegetables making a striking composition. When you actually stand in its midst, the illusion of beauty vanishes. Then you are assailed by the pungent odors of an Indian market, and the squalor and confusion can be overwhelming. But human interest is never lacking. Women do most of the selling, and there is a constant buzz of conversation. The men amble through the market place, lords of leisure for one day after the week's labor.

Corn and beans and lengths of bright cloth are heaped on the ground for market customers.

MEXICAN
CHRISTMAS:
BREAKING
THE PINATA

THE festival spirit that bubbles gaily on the weekly market days in Mexico boils up in a frenzy of color, song and dance for the nine days preceding Christmas. This is the supreme holiday time in a land devoted to holiday merrymaking. Starting on the 16th of December there is a procession each evening until the final one that takes place on Christmas Eve. Adults and children, all carrying lighted candles, form a line and march around the plaza or down a darkened street singing verse after verse of a song that tells how Mary and Joseph sought lodgings in Bethlehem. The procession stops in front of the closed door of a house or church, asking for admittance. When one of the singers announces that she is Mary, Queen of Heaven, the door is opened and the procession, including children who carry a flower-decked litter with images of the Holy Family, are permitted to enter.

After prayers and songs, the people crowd into the patio for refreshments and dancing. The celebration is called a *posada* (*poh*-SAH-*dah*), the Spanish word for lodging, because it commemorates the nine-days' search for shelter by the Holy Family. The climax of each evening's fun comes with the breaking of the *piñata* (*pee*-NYAH-*tah*). This is a clay jar decorated with brightly colored paper and filled with candies and toys. It is suspended from a rope, and someone is blindfolded, given a cane, and expected to whack the *piñata* hard enough to shatter it so that its gifts will rain down on the eager guests below. At such a moment, as you can see, the sombrero becomes a useful object for catching a fair share of the loot.

Mexico itself is like a giant *piñata* holding potential riches just out of reach of its people. But with increasing industrialization and the postwar economic boom, it is possible that the *piñata* will be broken at last, to shower its blessings on the patient and highhearted people of this colorful land.

SOME IMPORTANT DATES IN MEXICAN HISTORY

c. 15,000 B.C.	*First migration of Asiatic peoples to the New World. Crossed Bering Strait to Alaska, moved south. Some settled in Mexico.*
c. 160 A.D.-1500	*Mayan civilization rises and flourishes in Guatemala and later in peninsula of Yucatán.*
c. 900-1100	*The Toltec Indians dominate the central Valley of Mexico, near Teotihuacán, which later became the capital of the Aztec Empire.*
c. 1100-1521	*Aztec Empire dominates Mexico. Subjugates other Indian nations.*
1519	*Hernán Cortés lands in Veracruz and sets up first Spanish colony in Mexico, later called New Spain.*
1521	*Cortés conquers the Aztec Empire.*
1523-1821	*Mexico administered by Spain. Colonial period in Mexico brings subjugation of the Indian. Spain grows rich on wealth of Mexico's natural resources.*
Sept. 16, 1810	*In the town of Dolores, Father Miguel Hidalgo y Costilla issues his Grito of revolt. This is Mexican Independence Day, though revolutionists were defeated in 1811.*
1821	*General Agustin de Iturbide negotiates peace settlement with the Mexican revolutionary leader, Vicente Guerrero. Promises freedom for Mexico. Final break with Spain. Iturbide becomes head of Mexican Empire.*
1821-1876	*Seventy-four different governments in Mexico during this period.*
1846-1848	*Mexican-American War. United States defeats Mexican forces under General Santa Anna, and gains Texas and other territory.*
1854-1855	*The Revolution of Ayutla deposes the "perpetual dictator" Santa Anna, and starts reforms in Mexico.*
1857	*New constitution, written under liberal President Benito Juárez, heralds period of change.*
1864	*Internal wars and ill-planned reform measures lead to bankruptcy and European intervention. France, under Napoleon III, installs Maximilian and Carlotta as the heads of the new Mexican Empire.*
1867	*France withdraws her support of the Empire, Maximilian court-martialed and executed. Juárez returns to power.*
1871	*Porfirio Díaz leads a revolt against Juárez and has himself installed as president. Regime lasts until 1911.*
1910-1911	*Francisco I. Madero leads a successful revolt against the despotic regime of Díaz.*
1916-1917	*Following a raid into New Mexico, a punitive expedition is led by General Pershing, who attempts to capture Pancho Villa.*
1917	*Carranza president. New constitution sets forth labor code, agrarian and religious reforms, national ownership of subsoil deposits.*
1920-1934	*Revolutionary reorganization under Obregón and Calles.*
1942	*President Comacho declares war on the Axis powers.*
1946	*Miguel Alemán is post-war president, under whose regime many hopes of the revolution are realized. Country has prospered, government stabilized.*

SOME FAMOUS NAMES IN MEXICAN HISTORY

MONTEZUMA (1466-1520)—*Aztec Emperor, captured by Cortés, later killed in an Aztec uprising against the Spanish. Succeeded for a short time by nephew, Cuauhtemoc.*

HERNAN CORTES (1485-1547)—*Spanish conqueror of Mexico.*

ANTONIO DE MENDOZA (1485?-1552)—*First Viceroy of New Spain.*

SOR JUANA INES DE LA CRUZ (1651-1695)—*Mexican poetess, generally considered greatest lyric poet of the colonial period.*

MIGUEL HIDALGO Y COSTILLA (1753-1811)—*Mexican priest and revolutionary hero. Issued the Grito de Dolores (the Cry from Dolores), which roused the Mexican people to revolt against the Spanish in 1810. Killed in 1811 before he was able to see the dream of independence fulfilled.*

ANTONIO LOPEZ DE SANTA ANNA (1795?-1876)—*General who fought against the U.S. in Texas and was responsible for Alamo massacre. Became president of Mexico in 1833. Was dictator until 1855.*

BENITO JUAREZ (1806-1872)—*Full-blooded Zapotec Indian from Oaxaca. Elected president in 1861, started broad program of land and economic reforms. Forced to turn the government over to Maximilian in 1864. Juárez re-elected after empire fell in 1867.*

FERDINAND MAXIMILIAN (1832-1867) — *Austrian Archduke who accepted crown of the newly formed Mexican Empire from Napoleon III. In 1867 captured by Mexicans and executed at Querétaro.*

PORFIRIO DIAZ (1830-1915)—*Soldier, revolutionary, and president, 1877-1880 and 1884-1911. First rose to prominence in support of Juárez.*

FRANCISCO I. MADERO (1873-1913)—*With the aid of Pancho Villa and Emiliano Zapata, Madero overthrew Díaz dictatorship. First Mexican president chosen by completely free election in 1911. Launched the Revolution.*

FRANCISCO (PANCHO) VILLA (1877-1923)—*Revolutionary general and notorious bandit. Idol of Mexican masses, romanticized in ballads and tales.*

EMILIANO ZAPATA (1877?-1919)—*Mexican Indian who, with Madero, led movement of reform. Later fought Madero when he believed land reform was being ignored. His movement—"zapatismo"—advocated giving the land to the people.*

JOSE CLEMENTE OROZCO (1883-1949)—*One of the leaders of the Mexican artistic Renaissance. Gave new expression to the ancient mural form. One mural decorates the New School for Social Research in New York.*

DIEGO RIVERA (1886-1957)—*One of Mexico's greatest artists. Murals now decorate walls of the National Palace and the Palace of Fine Arts in Mexico City, the Palace of Cortés in Cuernavaca and many other buildings.*

LAZARO CARDENAS (1895-   )—*General and political leader. President of Mexico from 1934-40. His administration notable for land redistribution, expropriation of foreign-owned oil properties, development of industry and transportation.*

ADOLFO LOPEZ MATEOS (1910-   )—*President of Mexico, elected in 1958 to succeed Adolfo Ruiz Cortines.*

GUSTABO DIAZ-ORDAZ (1911–   )—*President of Mexico, elected in 1964.*

SOME SPANISH PHRASES AND WORDS

Do you speak English?   ¿Habla Usted inglés? (AH-*blah* oos-TEHD *een*-GLEHS)

How do you say . . . ?   ¿Cómo se dice . . . ? (KOH-*moh seh* DEE-*seh* . . .)

Can you help me?   ¿Puede Usted ayudarme? (PWEH-*deh* oos-TEHD *ah-yoo*-DAHR-*meh*)

I do not understand.   No comprendo. (*noh kohm*-PREHN-*doh*)

What do you wish?   ¿Qué desea Usted? (*keh deh*-SEH-*ah* oos-TEHD)

(Many) thanks.   (Muchas) gracias. (MOO-*chahs* GRAH-*syahs*)

You are welcome.   No hay de qué. (*noh eye deh keh*)

How much is it?   ¿Cuánto es? (KWAHN-*toh ehs*)

Why? What?   ¿Por qué? (*pohr keh*)   ¿Qué? (*keh*)

Who? When?   ¿Quien? (*kyehn*)   ¿Cuándo? (KWAHN-*doh*)

Yes. No.   Sí (*see*)   No (*noh*)

Perhaps.   Puede ser (PWEH-*deh sehr*)

Hello (good day).   Buenos días (BWEH-*nohs* DEE-*ahs*)

Goodbye.   Adiós (*ah*-DYOHS)

I am very glad to meet you.   Me alegro de conocerle. (*meh ah*-LEH-*groh deh koh-noh*-SEHR-*leh*)

    or less formally: Mucho gusto (MOO-*choh* GOOS-*toh*)

Where is it?   ¿Dónde está? (DOHN-*deh ehs*-TAH)

Ladies' room   Damas (DAH-*mahs*) *or* Señoras (*seh*-NYOH-*rahs*) *or* Mujeres (*moo*-HEH-*rehs*)

Men's room   Caballeros (*kah-bah*-LYEH-*rohs*) *or* Señores (*seh*-NYOH-*rehs*) *or* Hombres (OHM-*brehs*)

Airplane   Airport   El avión (*ehl ah*-VYOHN)   El aeropuerto (*ehl ah-eh-roh*-PWEHR-*toh*)

Bus   Train   El autobús (*ehl ah-oo-toh*-BOOS)   El tren (*ehl trehn*)

Boat   Baggage   El barco (*ehl* BAHR-*koh*)   El equipaje (*ehl eh-kee*-PAH-*heh*)

Hotel   Station   El hotel (*ehl oh*-TEHL)   La estación (*lah ehs-tah*-SYOHN)

DAYS OF THE WEEK: Los días de la semana (*lohs* DEE-*ahs deh lah seh*-MAH-*nah*)

Monday   Lunes (LOO-*nehs*)

Tuesday   Martes (MAHR-*tehs*)

Wednesday   Miércoles (MYEHR-*koh-lehs*)

Thursday   Jueves (HWEH-*vehs*)

Friday   Viernes (VYEHR-*nehs*)

Saturday   Sábado (SAH-*bah-doh*)

Sunday   Domingo (*doh*-MEEN-*goh*)

Today   Yesterday   Hoy (*oy*)   Ayer (*ah*-YEHR)

Tonight   Esta noche (EHS-*tah* NOH-*cheh*)

Tomorrow   Mañana (*mah*-NYAH-*nah*)

Week   Month   La semana (*lah seh*-MAH-*nah*)   El mes (*ehl mehs*)

Year   El año (*ehl* AH-*nyoh*)

NUMBERS: Números (NOO-*meh-rohs*)

One	Uno (OO-*noh*)		Seven	Siete (SYEH-*teh*)
Two	Dos (*dohs*)		Eight	Ocho (OH-*choh*)
Three	Tres (*trehs*)		Nine	Nueve (NWEH-*veh*)
Four	Cuatro (KWAH-*troh*)		Ten	Diez (*dyehs*)
Five	Cinco (SEEN-*koh*)		One hundred	Cien (*syehn*)
Six	Seis (SEH-*ees*)		One thousand	Mil (*meel*)

MONEY: El dinero (*ehl dee*-NEH-*roh*)

Peso (PEH-*soh*)

Centavo (*sen*-TAH-*voh*)=1/100 of a peso

INDEX